WHAT PEOPLE ARE SAYING

"An incredibly useful book! A step-by-step blueprint which gives you all the information you need to build a healthy, loving extended family."

Nick Ruben, Attorney, and Author of
How to Be a World-Class Listener

"I loved what I read. The book is a delightful mix of philosophy and information from a variety of sources blended with personal family experiences, packed in with practical 'hands on' tips on how to achieve peace within your family unit and ultimately yourself. It's a delicious book."

**Roz Carson, Teacher, Masters in
Psychoeducational Processes**

"I really enjoyed reading this book. It truly has had me thinking about how I can cultivate family ties."

Sue Wenger, Teacher

"Our people found it substantial and inspiring. Good Work!"
**John Brendler, Family Therapist, Founder of Building
Bridges, and Co-author of *Madness, Chaos, and
Violence: Therapy with Families at the Brink***

"I thought this was a great read!! I felt personally challenged by Steps 2 and 3. I want to be a better person, husband, father, brother, and uncle. I think many, many people will be blessed by what John and Sallie Raezer have written."

Tim Neils

The Celebrating Family

The Celebrating Family

Your Spiritual Roadmap to Family Healing and Happiness

JOHN AND SALLIE RAEZER

Published by Stewart Eckert Press

To contact the authors about speaking, consulting,
or ordering books in bulk, visit TheCelebratingFamily.com

ISBN (paperback): 979-8-9882333-0-5
ISBN (ebook): 979-8-9882333-1-2

Edited by Valerie Costa
Cover and Book Design by Christy Day,
Constellation Book Services

Printed in the United States of America

For James, Kara, Laurie, John, and Julie,
each one a gift from God.

Contents

Foreword

John and Sallie Raezer have produced a groundbreaking book about family bonding. Every year, forty-five family members enjoy a six-hour-long Christmas party and several other get-togethers, and trips. In beautiful detail, the Raezers describe family activities such as members speaking to the group about their past, future, and, importantly, their present moment. The family members celebrate their time together by singing songs (including the Raezer fight song, "The Holy City"), eating great dishes of all varieties, introducing innovative recipes discovered, researched, and tested, and emphasizing family spirituality in augmenting closeness.

Some of the Raezers' principles of family bonding include being there for one another, cooperating, forgiving, healing, celebrating, listening, serving, and sharing responsibilities. The goals of the energetic work of this project are to promote the development of a healthy family (excellent support for ill members), an emotionally strong family, kindness, and love. As judged by attendance and engagement, the project is a resounding success.

Not only is family bonding achieved, but this work (and fun) could become a model for other families, and family therapy. Schools and classes within schools might encourage bonding by applying some of the principles and activities clearly described in this book. Many churches and Sunday schools could use these ideas. Book clubs and other groups might implement aspects of this model that are appropriate in their context. Neighborhoods, villages, small towns (and larger ones), small and large businesses, governmental entities, and different organizations may adapt the ideas to their particular needs.

The most immediate clinical use could be as part of family therapy. Families can benefit from more attachment, kindness, and love. Skilled psychotherapists may bring creative activities, music, and food, as well, to their process. Therapy, in general today, may have too many analytic and intellectual components rather than positive affective elements.

The useful bonding strategies that the Raezers have presented—celebration, travel, tradition, affection, outings, and support—can be emphasized by therapists in addition to standard approaches. John and Sallie have given us a set of practical tools with which we can enhance the lives of families and various other groups.

–Arthur M. Freeman III, M.D.
Clinical Professor of Psychiatry,
Tulane University School of Medicine
Former Dean, LSU Medical Center, Shreveport

Introduction

Do you feel distanced from a family member? Are there family members you don't speak to? Does your family fight when they get together? Does anyone remember your birthday? Do you spend the holidays alone?

Can you envision the joy of closeness instead of isolation? Can you imagine family parties that are full of fun and laughter? Do you wish to have an exciting, connected family life?

If you answered 'yes' to any of these questions, you want what we call a Celebrating Family, where family members love spending time together on a regular basis. Get-togethers tighten family bonds, the deep-rooted connections people have to one another.

Creating a Celebrating Family is not a matter of happenstance or luck. You need a great game plan that you can execute. Our 8-Step Program presents the required skills and principles that will transform your family into one that works together as a team. Learn the strategies that promote bonding and love. You will be able to plan family events that will produce special memories and ultimately celebrations. Our mission is to provide you with the concepts, tools, and methodology to fulfill your dream of a bonded Celebrating Family.

Why did we write this book? Its genesis came from conversations with friends about our annual family Christmas party. When hearing us talk glowingly about this event, many responded by asking, "How is it possible that you have gotten forty to fifty members of your family together every year for twenty years when so many live far away? You need to write a book to tell us what you did."

One event in particular helped motivate us. Our nephew mentioned to his employer that he would be taking a day off to attend our Christmas party. His boss angrily told him that if he did, he would lose his job. Our nephew responded that attending the party was far more important than keeping the job. Happily, his boss was so impressed with his devotion to family that he relented. On hearing about this, we were so moved by his actions that we decided to explore writing a book about celebrating families.

We asked ourselves, "Can we explain what we have done to create a family that really wants to spend time together and replicate it for other families to use?"

We had, behind us, extensive exposure to family therapy and decades of experience working with people as we designed software systems. With these backgrounds, we felt uniquely positioned to develop a universal framework for families to achieve the goal of having a Celebrating Family.

Throughout his youth, John witnessed those who, when angry, responded with physical and verbal outbursts. His family's get-togethers were a battleground for airing old grudges and creating new ones. One Thanksgiving, a family member hit John in the face. His father threw his brother-in-law out the front door and later knocked down the door to recover his belongings after divorcing his mother.

Unfortunately, John had internalized the behaviors around him. During his senior year in high school, he punched a basketball referee who charged him with three fouls in very quick succession. Suddenly he was in danger of being thrown out of high school sports and was told that his actions would be reported to Harvard, where he had just been accepted. Everything he had worked for was at risk. He had reached a low point but didn't know how to stop the madness. It was only through the intervention of his football coach that he was permitted to attend Harvard. He continued to dig deeper holes, which included two divorces, and it would be many decades before he was able to reach a state of inner peace.

Sallie also knows broken family relationships. She divorced her first husband and experienced a separation from family members for a long period of time. She understands the pain of broken bonds and has lived the importance of forgiveness.

Together, John and Sallie have created a step-by-step guide to help other families achieve what they have come to cherish in their family. They now have a Celebrating Family and, in this book, they share the eight steps that changed their lives.

This is not a psychology book. It is not a book about healing addictions, overcoming childhood traumas, or combatting mental illness. It is not a book that counsels those getting a divorce. It is a book that looks at the family as a team and tells you what the team needs to master to win. It provides the tools for becoming a Celebrating Family.

This book is predicated on the belief that there exists a higher power, and from that higher power comes a set of vital, life-changing moral principles. John and Sallie embraced the thinking of several major philosophers. Meister Eckhart of the thirteenth century said that it is only from divine grace that humans derive their worth. He believed that the spiritual world was the real world, and that spiritual debate always trumps political debate. Immanuel Kant of the seventeenth century believed in man's inherent desire to do good and the moral principles, or as he called it, The Categorical Imperative, that logically flow out of this desire. These principles are universally accepted because they are seen as good. They are manifested in 'Do unto others as you would have them do unto you,' otherwise known as the Golden Rule. Alexis de Tocqueville of the nineteenth century identified the family as the strength of America. In America, he found marriages based on love and families with good morals. America offered social mobility and the opportunity for advancement for those who were willing to work, today called the pursuit of the American Dream. The American Dream includes having a Celebrating Family.

It is now time to build the team that will help you transform your family. Step 1 will get you started. Let's see what love can do!

The Benefits of a Celebrating Family

As a member of a Celebrating Family, you love spending time together because you feel:

- ➤ **Respected.** You are treated with dignity and warmly welcomed to each event.

- ➤ **Valued.** When you are unable to attend, you will be missed.

- ➤ **Listened to.** You know that others will listen patiently.

- ➤ **Understood.** You know that other family members will try hard to understand you.

- ➤ **Supported.** You know that in times of trouble, family members will be there for you.

- ➤ **Trusted.** Members know that you are a person of your word.

- ➤ **Loved.** Members demonstrate love through their words and actions.

Overview of Your 8-Step Program

Step 1. Build Your Team

Step 2. Master the Skills that Demonstrate Respect for Others

> ➢ Learn to Be on Time
>
> ➢ Learn to Listen Well
>
> ➢ Learn to Honor Your Commitments
>
> ➢ Learn to Be Fair
>
> ➢ Learn to Express Gratitude

Step 3. Adopt the Principles that Demonstrate Love for Others

> ➢ Be There for One Another
>
> ➢ Cooperate with One Another

- ➢ Forgive One Another
- ➢ Heal One Another
- ➢ Empathize with One Another
- ➢ Serve One Another
- ➢ Hug One Another

Step 4. Explore Family Bonding Strategies

- ➢ Remember Birthdays
- ➢ Attend/Host Individuals' Events
- ➢ Give Meaningful Gifts
- ➢ Host Family Parties
- ➢ Take Family Trips
- ➢ Take Trips for Two
- ➢ Attend Sponsored Walks
- ➢ Attend Entertainment Events
- ➢ Explore Genealogy

Step 5. Review Bonding Strategies that Work for You

- ➢ Individual Member's Event Moments
- ➢ Gift Moments

- Family Party Moments
- Family Trip Moments
- Trips for Two Moments
- Sponsored Walk Moments
- Entertainment Event Moments
- Genealogy Exploration Moments

Step 6. Master Event-Planning Skills

- Learn to Set a Date and Send Invitations
- Learn to Prepare and Purchase Delicious Food
- Learn to Select Engaging Music
- Learn to Select Games
- Learn to Conduct Circle Time
- Learn to Toast

Step 7. Establish an Annual Family Party Event

- Select Activities
- Plan the Schedule
- Plan the Menu
- Plan the Music

➤ Share the Work

➤ Share the Costs

Step 8. Gather Feedback About Your Annual Event and Implement Improvements

STEP 1

Build Your Team

When we say "family" in this book, we mean the fully extended family, the whole family tree. Most families tell us they have siblings or cousins or an uncle or parents that they are not on speaking terms with. Most would prefer that that weren't so and would like to begin the work of repairing their family. Before you begin this work, however, you need to build your team, as you cannot do this alone.

You probably have an idea who might be receptive to your objective of a Celebrating Family. This is the place to start. Call or visit as many family members as you can. Show them the list of benefits and the overview of the eight-step program presented at the beginning of this book and determine who wants to be on the team. If you experience resistance, don't push them. Move on. Embrace those who are enthusiastic about starting the journey. Aim to have at least two households represented to get started.

Resistance can take many forms. Some are simply unsure and will be glad to join events when they hear that they are working well. Others are content with the brokenness and don't want to put any energy into changing it. Even so, there is still hope. Unforeseen and unplanned events like a serious car accident or a near-fatal heart attack can soften hearts and foster a desire for connection. You need to be patient; some will join later.

Love will transform your family.

STEP 2

Master the Skills That Demonstrate Respect for Others

When you begin the process of transforming a family to be a celebrating one, you need to establish an environment of respect for others. The Golden Rule says, "Do unto others as you would have them do unto you."

Everyone wants to be treated well. The skills you need to accomplish this are discussed in this chapter:

> ➤ Learn to Be on Time

> ➤ Learn to Listen Well

> ➤ Learn to Honor Your Commitments

> ➤ Learn to Be Fair

> ➤ Learn to Express Gratitude

Learn to Be on Time

Those who wish to honor others arrive on time. Being punctual shows consideration for the host, who has carefully planned the event's timeline. When guests don't arrive as expected, it causes the host to question how to accommodate those who are running late. Do we wait? Do we hold off putting the entrée in the oven? Do we put our plan on hold until we know what they are doing? Depending on the size of the party, adjustments may not be practical. As the host, don't adjust for the chronic offender.

Being on time takes advance planning. Make sure you have the correct address of your destination and a phone number in case you need to call. Google Maps or a similar map application will calculate the mileage and time that it takes to drive from your location to the event. Add a small buffer of time for something to take longer than expected. If it is a long trip, budget time for rest stops and snacks. If the weather forecast is poor, add additional time. Calculate the departure time that will get you to the event on time. If something unforeseen happens to cause you to be late, alert your host as soon as possible.

If you are habitually tardy, change your preparation. Perhaps you are leaving too much to do on the day of the event. If a gift needs to be purchased and/or wrapped, do this ahead of time. You might want to put a reminder on the calendar to complete this the weekend before. If you are bringing food, prepare or purchase it ahead of time. Set out your clothes the night before. Set an alarm so you don't oversleep. Being habitually late is very disruptive and can be overcome with good planning.

Learn to Listen Well

The goal of listening well is to build understanding of another family member. Take the time to understand someone fully and they will feel deeply valued. In his book, *How to Be a World-Class Listener*, Nick Ruben wrote that when you really listen to someone, it's like giving a gift of pure oxygen that will cause people to open up like flowers in the sun.

There are many things you can do to become a great listener. Show your interest by asking questions. Avoid questions that require a yes or no answer. Instead, ask, "How did you feel about that?" or "What was it like?"

Allow them to complete their thoughts, making sure that they are finished talking before you jump in. Along with not interrupting, your curiosity will make them feel cared about.

Ask them to repeat anything that you are not clear about. When you reach an understanding, you may not agree on every point and that is okay. Politics can be a cause that separates, but family harmony must take precedence over political position. It is better to agree to disagree respectfully than press to be right. Don't quibble about wording. Look for what is being said that you can agree with. If being right is more important than being vulnerable, communication becomes a trial rather than an adventure in learning and loving.

Generally, most of our statements land appropriately, meaning that what we intended to say is received the way we intended it. Sometimes, though, the impact can be far different from what was meant. We can hear something that upsets us. When this occurs, it is very effective to say, "The impact of what you said was this. Was that your intent?" More often than not, they will respond by saying, "Oh no, I misspoke. What I meant to say was something different." This will stop a misunderstanding before it starts.

We have all been in discussions where someone wants to do all the talking. That same person will interrupt and talk over others. Someone must kindly point out that everyone needs a chance to be heard.

Try something new if communication is stuck. Sallie and John had a recurring discussion that they couldn't seem to resolve. Sallie said, "Since we are not getting anywhere, I am going to look up our Myers-Briggs personality testing results from long ago to see if they will shed some light on our communication styles."

This personality test is based on the psychologist Carl Jung's theory of personality types. Using a set of multiple-choice questions, the tool categorizes you into one of sixteen types, and explains what it means. We read the reports together and promptly started laughing. Sallie's strength is getting the overview, and John's strength is in the detail. John had fallaciously assumed that women focus on details and men on the big picture. It was an aha moment that led to much-needed change in their marriage. Now they divide the work more appropriately based on their strengths, as they know who is more comfortable with certain types of assignments. When they talk about an issue, they focus on whether they are talking about details or the big picture. With a creative new approach and good information, they resolved a very stuck conversation.

In his book, *Emotional Intelligence*, Daniel Goleman describes an emotionally hijacked person as one who has had an overwhelmingly emotional reaction to something that causes them to lose the ability to reason and listen for a period of time. You must recognize when someone close to you has become emotionally hijacked. Recently, Sallie said she was going to the emergency room. The mention of an ER visit triggered John to relive a frightening experience with their daughter, Julie, in an ER a year earlier. John insisted that Sallie not go. Sallie knew that his reasoning wasn't based on her needs, and she took herself to the ER the next day. She had had a concussion and was experiencing scary symptoms. If you find yourself in a conversation with someone who is emotionally hijacked, understand that he or she should not be making decisions.

Karl Menninger said that we move towards those who listen well to us, and that this has a way of creating us and making us expand. When your family members become excellent listeners, it will go a long way to build the strong family bonds that you are seeking.

Learn to Honor Your Commitments

Every day we are asked to commit to doing things. You become a "person of your word" if you do what you say you will do when you say you will do it. This is the reputation you want to build, and it means that you honor your commitments. Doing what you promise to do will help build a strong family.

People make plans around what you have committed to do. Valid reasons do come up that can affect what you are doing, but that should be a rare exception. When this happens, inform the affected party as soon as possible. Broken commitments can be like dominoes. They may mean the next person can't deliver and then the next.

Do you often have to apologize for breaking your promises? If the answer is yes, we suggest assessing the process you go through to make commitments.

First, you need to be very clear about what is being asked of you. Is the request reasonable? Is it something you can do, and do you have enough time to do it? You must decide what you are capable of and commit sensibly rather than not be able to deliver. This applies to commitments both large and small. Recently, Sallie was asked to bring her homemade cheesecake to a family gathering but knew she didn't have the time to prepare such a complicated recipe that week. She elected to purchase a cake instead. People often do not know how much work they are asking you to do. Make sure to say no to assignments that are not practical for you.

Second, write down what you have promised to do and when you need to deliver it. Sallie uses her iPhone calendar to record what is due on a certain date. She also sets enough time aside on her calendar to do the required work. This approach will remind you with enough warning to successfully keep your promises.

Family trust is built by honoring your commitments. The old axiom that "actions speak louder than words" rings true. John's mother reminded her three sons that talk is cheap. All sizes of commitments matter, and as Carl Jung said so eloquently, "You are what you do, not what you say you'll do."

Learn to Be Fair

Fairness embodies a commitment to playing by the rules and acting in ways that do not seek to take advantage of others. Brit Hume was accurate when he said that fairness is an expertise that needs to be mastered.

If someone cheats to win, the game isn't fun.

Our daughter, Julie, coached American teenagers competing in tennis tournaments in Europe for a couple of summers. Julie was familiar with events in the U.S. where each player called their own lines, often unfairly. She found line calls to be problematic in Europe as well, until she and her players arrived in the Netherlands. The tournament rules there were different. If you won a match, you were obligated to buy a soft drink for your opponent and spend an hour chatting together. Players did not cheat knowing that they would be socializing afterwards.

No matter what game you are playing, make sure your ego does not depend on the outcome. It is just a game, and your opponent is a real person with feelings. Make sure you treat them the way you would want to be treated: fairly. Play by the rules. Win and lose graciously.

Family members often play games together. Games provide a great opportunity to teach children about taking turns and playing by the rules. The roll of the dice is something we cannot control, and we all need to accept that there are times when they don't roll in our favor.

Games teach us where skills and strategies can be improved and how to win and lose with grace. Families need to stand for fairness and model it for their children. If someone in the family always must go first or always takes the best equipment or always eats the best cookies, this is not fair. Even young children can understand if there are enough cookies for everyone to have only one, then one person must not take two.

Going out for a meal with a group is a great opportunity to teach fairness. There are those who always order the most courses and the most expensive entrée and then suggest splitting the bill. There are those who, mindful that they overspent others, will throw in an extra amount to be fair when the tab is divvied up. Make sure that you have covered your own bill. People will know if they felt fairly treated.

Some children grow up feeling that they are not the favorite child. Unfavored status can mean receiving less attention. It can mean feeling unentitled where a sibling is entitled. It may mean that you always get what is left over and unwanted. Feeling less equal can lead to bad outcomes down the road. Parents need to eliminate their propensity for favoritism to have a healthy family.

Fair must not be confused with equal. You need to provide glasses for a child that needs them to function. You wouldn't purchase them for the sibling who doesn't have a similar requirement. Perhaps that child needs a tutor. As a parent, you are seeking to provide support wherever it is needed.

Everyone makes mistakes. Those who handle it well own their actions, apologize, and do whatever is needed to fix the situation. Others look for reasons to blame everyone else. Admit when you are wrong. This is the fair thing to do.

Structure every agreement with family members such that you would be happy with either outcome. Both parties should see it as a "win-win." Win-losses are really a lose-lose and can seriously hurt relationships.

Fairness is fundamental to demonstrating respect for others.

Learn to Express Gratitude

A thank you can come in many different forms: in person, text, email, or handwritten notes. All are awesome to receive and go a long way to build solid relationships. Everyone needs to feel appreciated and valued. Johannes Gaertner summed it up well when he said that those who live gratitude touch heaven.

We all love it when someone mentions how much they appreciated something we did that helped them or that they loved the meal we made or the gift we sent. We all like to be on the receiving end of a statement of appreciation, but often don't think to be appreciative ourselves. Kenneth Blanchard advocates taking time to recognize positive acts and writes about this in his book, *Catch a Person Doing Something Right.* Celebrating an act confirms that it felt loving and built trust. The more positive actions that are celebrated, the stronger the group becomes. Encourage family members to look for opportunities to express gratitude and role model this behavior.

When Sallie closes her eyes at night, she thinks of ten things that have blessed her that day or in recent days. For her, this practice fosters an attitude of appreciation. The exercise often reminds her that she has not yet thanked someone for an act of kindness.

Jean-Baptiste Alphonse Karr said, "There are people who complain that roses have thorns; I, on the other hand, appreciate that thorns have roses." We can focus on what is negative or what is positive. We each get to decide which lens we want to look through to view our world.

Dr. Martin Seligman, in his book *Authentic Happiness*, recounted how he asked each student in his Positive Psychology course to invite a guest to class who had been important in their lives but whom they had never properly thanked. Proper thank yous were delivered on Gratitude Night, apparently with no dry eyes in the room. Dr.

Seligman said, "So dramatic was the impact of Gratitude Night that it did not require an experiment to convince me of its power."

We suggest that those who have never focused their efforts on gratitude begin today. Notice an act of kindness, express your appreciation, and then note the positive impact on the other person. This practice will build a beautiful heart.

STEP 3

Adopt the Principles That Demonstrate Love for Others

In addition to mastering the skills that indicate respect for others, a transforming family will need to accept the moral principles that demonstrate love for other people. These principles are the focus of this chapter:

- ➤ Be There for One Another

- ➤ Cooperate with One Another

- ➤ Forgive One Another

- ➤ Heal One Another

- ➤ Empathize with One Another

- ➤ Serve One Another

- ➤ Hug One Another

Be There for One Another

The number one principle that demonstrates our love is to be there for one another. Being there takes many forms. As relationships typically have a rhythm, it is important to check in regularly. "Regularly" can be defined differently for different relationships. Some parents call their children at college once a week. Some families of grown children schedule a family dinner every week. Some adult siblings text each other every day. There are no rules other than to stay connected.

Sometimes an unexpected call informs you that a family member's well-being is at risk. Perhaps he or she had a heart attack and was rushed to the hospital or was in a serious car accident. These types of crises are never predictable, but family responses are. We need to do whatever it takes to make these family members feel our support and love. One of the main drivers of recovery is a caring family.

Being There When You Can't Be Present

When Sallie's mom was moved to a dementia care unit many states away, Sallie struggled with how to "be there" for her. The facility where Mom lived had a private kitchen area that families could use. Many times, we packed a cooler of breakfast ingredients and jumped into the car on Saturday mornings at 4 a.m. The early start permitted us to serve breakfast to Mom at the time she usually ate. The time together was special, but it was not practical to make the trip very often.

Longing for more time together, Sallie tried singing with Mom during their phone calls. She placed her cell phone on the piano, put it on speaker, and played the piano. They sang Mom's favorite songs together. They ended each call with, "I love you, Mom." "I love you, Sallie." One day Sallie could no longer hear Mom singing at the other end of the phone and was worried. She called the home and was told that Mom was silently mouthing all the words. "Please keep calling her," they said.

And so, she did. But Sallie had experienced a great loss and sometimes had to fight back tears while singing.

Then Sallie was told that Mom was approaching her last days. She drove to her home and sat by her side. Mom was breathing but was completely unresponsive. Sallie began singing her favorite songs and saw Mom's paralyzed mouth struggle to form a smile. There was deep connection between them. Mom passed away soon after that. Sallie was so grateful she and her mother had remained close despite the physical distance.

Christmas With Our Son and His Family in Germany

There have been holidays that we haven't been able to be physically with our son and his family in Germany. We wanted so much to be there. He sent gifts to us ahead of time and we to his family. On Christmas Eve, we opened gifts 'together' with a laptop set up so we could share the moment. It was a great solution.

Providing Support Before, During, and After Major Surgery

In July 2015, our daughter, Julie, was diagnosed with a malignant brain tumor. During her eight-hour surgery to remove the tumor, we sat in the brain surgery family waiting room at Jefferson's Neuroscience Hospital in Philadelphia. Many families were there, but we were the only ones blessed to have company to lighten our burden. Julie's future husband Brad, our son John's future wife, Carolin, and two dear friends waited with us for news from the surgeon.

The surgeon was able to remove most of the tumor, but in doing so, Julie's right side was paralyzed. She would require months of chemotherapy and three weeks of in-house rehabilitation to learn to walk again. She did not recover use of her right hand.

Her brother John was on a business trip to the Philippines while this was going on. Carolin arranged to meet him when his plane arrived at Kennedy International Airport so that she could gently explain what had happened to his beloved sister while he was away. We waited by Julie's bed for his arrival. It was a teary reunion.

Brad spent the week after Julie's surgery by her side, saying, "I can't concentrate at work with you like this." After returning to work, he drove long distances to see her every night. He sent flowers.

Julie's cousin brought ice cream to the hospital to share with her for breakfast. Yes, breakfast. He has received a commitment from Julie to return the "ice cream for breakfast" favor when and if he might ever need it.

Sallie's San Francisco cousins blessed us with a week of dinners from The Grateful Plate. We still think about how this lifted us up.

Throughout this tough time, we never felt alone. Our family and friends were there for us. Julie has since had two more brain surgeries and each time, our son, John, who is now living with his family in Germany, returned to be by his sister's side. His presence has been uplifting.

In February of 2003, at nine in the morning, Sallie thought her husband John, appeared to be suffering from a heart attack. She alerted his doctor, who then informed the hospital of his imminent arrival. Sallie promptly took him to the emergency room, where he underwent quintuple bypass surgery. His brother David waited with Sallie. Sallie's parents drove from Long Island to take care of Sallie and John's young children. John's older children, Jimmy, Kara, and Laurie also checked in. Everyone asked how they could help. John felt they all wrapped their arms around him and helped him through a difficult year-long recovery. Sallie's quick response saved his life.

In all instances, we did not experience these life changing events alone. There was always family support and love, the greatest medicine of all.

Cooperate With One Another

Everybody needs to pull their weight to make a family work. As none of us is self-sufficient, we depend on the support of others. Is there something that your family needs done that could be your responsibility?

When John and his two brothers were very young, their father handed each of them a stick and asked them to break it. All three did it easily. He then handed each a bundle of three sticks and once again asked them to break it. This time they failed. The point of the exercise was to convince them that family life will be more joyous if they work together rather than compete with one another. While they later learned that this was Aesop's fable and not their father's, it made no difference; the power of the message remains. Sallie and John rejoice as more and more family members elect to cooperate, adding their sticks to the family bundle.

John was fortunate to have played football at Lower Merion High School for Coach John Fritz Brennan. Coach Brennan focused on the eleven players who worked best together, not the eleven best athletes. He emphasized teamwork over individual performance. John learned that the whole can be greater than the sum of the parts. When everyone tries to help each other, the family is a winning team.

Working with Our Daughter and Her Husband

We mentioned that our daughter, Julie, had brain surgery some years ago. She is now unable to drive and needs support with certain tasks. Brad works full time and can't do all that needs to be done to help her. We have elected to become part of their team. Every Monday through Friday, we review what needs to be done to help. Sallie plans doctors' visits, MRIs, and therapies and takes Julie shopping for clothing, shoes, pocketbooks, and gifts; whatever needs to be purchased at the moment. John is her "Uber driver" and drives her to therapy once a week and MRIs and whatever else is required. There are telehealth visits and in-person visits, and we accompany her to all of them.

Recently, Julie has been using an exoskeleton, or "bionic" arm, as we call it, to awaken muscles and fingers that have long atrophied, boosting them to move for the first time in years. It has been an entire family effort to get its technical intricacies understood and working effectively for her. As some sensitivity is returning to her fingers, our team scored a life-changing touchdown.

Sallie and John also take care of Brad and Julie's chihuahua mixed-breed dog, Jake, so that Brad and Julie can get away periodically. Jake is what we call a "love bug." Very sweet, except when he slipped under the backyard fence and couldn't be located for forty minutes. Happily, he has gained enough poundage that he is no longer a flight risk. Sallie and John have recovered from the concern he caused, and we are enjoying his visits.

Our mission has been to improve Julie and Brad's quality of life and we feel good when we are able to do that. Brad's expertise is technology, and we so appreciate it when he helps us with our computers. When he does this, he is demonstrating his concern for us, and we feel valued. Whenever Julie visits, she helps in every way she can.

Figure out what you can do to help other family members. Cooperate, don't compete, and you will strengthen your family.

Forgive One Another

Is there someone in your family you need to be reunited with? No principle plays a more significant role in keeping a family intact than forgiving one another.

Over the years, we have asked people about their families. Their most common response is that they have been separated from part of their family for a long time. They cite a litany of snubs and abuses. We ask them how this is working for them, and are told it doesn't work at all. They have been hurt and are stuck.

With forgiveness, this doesn't have to be the end of the story. Revisit the relationship. Be the first to forgive or ask for forgiveness. Forgiveness introduces "humanness" to a situation run amok. How powerful the benefits are to both the person who forgives and the person who has been forgiven. In the book, *Amish Grace*, a farmer warns of the dangers of the failure to forgive when he says that the acid of hate destroys the container. If forgiveness is not given, give the relationship some time and then bring the subject up again.

Forgiving a Sibling

There was a time when John and his brother Tom were at odds. John had started a management consulting company and asked Tom to be a partner. After many years, Tom wanted to take the firm in a different direction. John disagreed. So, Tom formed a new company and took several employees with him. The separation created a rift between the brothers. For several years, they and their families stopped seeing each other. During that time, the pain of loss of family was less than John's belief in having to be right. As time went on, however, this balance changed. John realized that being right was much less important than being together as brother and brother. He called Tom and told him he forgave him; Tom did likewise. It was this act of forgiveness, expressed in a time of high mutual vulnerability, that put their differences behind them. It gave new life to the family. When John and Tom forgave each other, a great cloud was lifted. They restored their relationship.

When families become fractured for whatever reason, the only way we believe to bring them back together is for the parties involved to forgive one another openly and completely; no strings attached. As William J. Powell said, it is our duty to forgive and heal the past and move on to a world that is hopeful because we made it that way.

Heal One Another

It is easy to complain about a family member's behavior, but what about instead thinking about the role you could play in fostering his or her growth? Sometimes when we suffer, we are too close to the situation to help ourselves. Do you have a loved one who is suffering? How could you help? Do you hold the key to changing their situation? Can you think of a loving way to step in that will leave them stronger?

Gaining Closure

"We never buried my father." John had said this many times before. In fact, Sallie had heard it for years, but this time she responded differently. "Where is he and why can't we bury him?"

John thought his ashes might be at a local funeral home. Sallie made several calls and quickly located the urn of the father-in-law she had never met. The surprised funeral director told her there would be a charge of $460 for Ottomer Raezer's remains, as they had been at the funeral parlor for twenty years. We paid the bill.

John and his brothers thought a lot about the type of burial their dad would want. Recalling their dad's love of Townsend's Inlet, the inlet between Longport and Ocean City, New Jersey, we chartered a boat with a captain. A large gathering of Raezers watched as the three brothers poured the precious ashes into the churning water. Afterward, we celebrated Dad's life over dinner at a nearby restaurant. It was a special day of closure.

Raising Awareness

Early in their marriage, John helped Sallie to become a better functioning human being in a profound way. She had been inexplicably and without warning shutting down in the middle of a conversation. We called it "pulling down the curtain."

When it occurred, she could be "gone" for a long time and wouldn't be able to explain what had happened. John said, "I will sit with you until you can tell me what is going on."

The first time it took about twenty-four hours to remember and then verbalize that the trigger had been something that hurt her. Each time, John waited patiently, insistent that Sallie speak about what had happened. Awareness came faster and faster until there was no time lag at all. Sallie was better and so thankful that her husband chose to love her in this way.

Solving the Cleaning Too Much Habit

"The Mad Wiper" was a nickname John had earned because he stood at the kitchen counter with one hand circling endlessly to clean a spot that could no longer have been there. No discussion changed this. No urging relaxed the habit.

One day, Sallie went to lunch with a friend who spoke of her children in this way. "One is attending Harvard and one is in high school, but both are being treated for obsessive compulsive disorder. They can't deal with their shoes."

Obvious parallels came to mind. John's shoestrings, always untied, flap dangerously as he walks. Is this what it means to "not be able to deal with your shoes?" Was John suffering from OCD?

Later that day, Sallie sat in a doctor's waiting room and noticed that all the books lined up over the mantle were about OCD. On the wall, an announcement of a meeting of a support group for OCD sufferers had been posted. A subject Sallie had never done much thinking about had, that day, become a throbbing variable.

In the ensuing months, Sallie read extensively about OCD and made calls to determine where to get the best help for her dear husband. He was, however, not on board with her plan. A neighbor changed that shortly.

John had all the doors of three cars open with trunks in the air. He was going from car to car, energetically vacuuming with a handheld. Their neighbor came running out of her home with her fist shaking. "What are you doing? Get back in the house. It is ninety-eight degrees, and you just had a heart attack."

He stopped instantly and appeared at our front door, asking, "Will you please get me help?"

These were the words Sallie had been waiting to hear. She made an appointment for John, and he was quickly freed from the prison of his compulsive behavior. He needed to be ready.

Pushing a Loved One to Exercise

When our daughter, Julie, was at Magee Rehabilitation Hospital relearning to walk after her first brain surgery, Brad pushed her to do her rehab exercises and to walk farther and longer than she could push herself. He loved her back to walking and back to work. Julie says, "Every girl needs a Bradley."

Fundamental to strong families is the well-being of its members. If we are listening for ways to help each other heal, we can often be the difference that our loved one needs.

Empathize with One Another

Matshona Dhiliwayo said that if you haven't walked in a person's shoes, you won't understand the sores on their feet. Being empathetic requires a sincere interest in understanding a person's history and ultimately how they think. Once a family member feels understood and valued, they are open to sharing and will embrace the bonding moments they experience when interacting with you. It is empathetic listening that builds trust, the precondition for bonding.

Every family member has a story. It is important to discover that story. Only then can you understand how they think, what they value, and what they need. Ask questions. At a minimum, these include where they grew up, how they felt growing up, whether they have brothers and sisters, where they went to school, and where they have worked.

Empathetic listening is particularly difficult when you are hearing things that you don't want to hear. You know you are an empathetic listener when you permit yourself to learn something new from the encounter. Thank the member for opening your eyes to new understandings. Empathetic listening is critical to family strength.

Listening to the Truth After Major Surgery and Embracing the Result

A test of our commitment to the principle of empathetic listening came after Julie had her brain surgery. Julie, who observes a lot but says little, started "to speak the truth." One of her first comments was that her dad cannot plan. When she was being transferred from Jefferson Hospital to Magee Rehabilitation, she announced that she could not depend on Dad to manage the move. If Mom were here, it would get done. All of which is true, but Dad never heard it articulated so succinctly and so dogmatically.

She also said that Dad and Uncle Dave think that the Raezer family produces great athletes. She felt, though, that Mom's family was the source of her athleticism. Her statement was later confirmed when John ran into his former high school basketball coach. John asked if he remembered him and reminded him that he had been his high school coach. He simply answered, "Tennis." John asked what he was talking about. He informed John that the only great Raezer athlete who attended Lower Merion was Julie Raezer. She was All-State First Team for four years, led her team to the state finals the four years she played, was second in the state in singles, and won the state doubles championship. John got a much-needed dose of reality about his athletic contributions to his high school and learned the importance of becoming an empathetic listener. Julie's observations often generated some laughter, but in the end were completely on target.

Adopting Cultural Traditions from Family Members

The principle of empathetic listening can lead to enhanced cultural understanding. Among the members of the Raezer family are men and women who were born in Italy, Canada,

Korea, and Germany. Each member has shared with the family new foods and traditions. Increased cultural understanding can lead to many moments of bonding. It is important that you understand the cultural background of each member and encourage them to share their family traditions and foods.

Empathetic listening opportunities are everywhere. Use them to enrich your family. Family members have within them experiences and traditions that can enhance family member understanding, family fun, and bonding. Use empathetic listening to mine new understandings. You will be so glad you did.

Serve One Another

It is important to teach our family members to use their gifts to serve others by lightening their burdens. Observing that someone has a need and bringing your gifts to serve that need is what serving others is all about. Shifting our focus from our own selves permits us to focus on those around us. Albert Schweitzer said that when we live for others, our lives may be more difficult, but are richer and happier.

Serving can come in the form of taking in boarders, delivering meals to the sick, lending a ride, or providing needed expertise. It is all about where you can help. The list of possibilities is restricted only by your imagination.

Martin Luther King, Jr. said that anyone can be great because they have the capacity to serve. He added that all you need is a heart full of grace and a soul generated by love. The benefits of serving others are enormous. In serving others, we learn to listen well, problem solve, and gain trust and understanding of one another. All family members will be better off if we are actively serving one another. Caring for and supporting others helps us to grow.

Taking in Boarders

Our pastor has often referred to our home as Raezer's Bed and Breakfast. While we are not actively seeking boarders, we do have a separate area with a bedroom, bathroom, and TV room that is private. It permits us to house family and friends who have a short-term need.

One family stayed with us when their upstairs bathroom leaked water into their kitchen, rendering both unusable. We asked if we could help, and they accepted. It was quite a while before the construction dust was gone and they could move back into their home. Another family had sold their home and had a short-term housing need before their home in Tennessee would become available. They filled in the gap at our home. One of our daughter's college friends lived with us for over a year. Not knowing if she would like the job she had accepted, she preferred to stay with us rather than commit to a lease. Our boarders enriched us.

Tutoring from Afar

About six months after Julie was married, she developed aphasia. Aphasia is a devastating condition. Julie was left struggling to speak, struggling to read, and struggling to write.

She hungered for help. Sallie worked to help her relearn the alphabet and numbers during the mornings. Sallie's cousin, Charlyn, who lives in Tennessee, wanted to help, as well. She and Julie have selected books to read, and practice reading by phone most afternoons. Thanks to Charlyn's loving support, Julie has greatly improved, and they have built a beautiful friendship along the way.

Learning the Importance of Service

John attended Ardmore Junior High. Every week in the auditorium, the principal gathered the students to tell a story. Each story contained a lesson in personal discipline, such as "be on time" and "polish your shoes in the back as well as the front." He taught them the importance of service. Service was so front and center in his thinking that engraved in the masonry block atop the entrance to Ardmore Junior High School were the words "Enter to Learn, Go Forth to Serve."

These words touched the hearts and minds of students, so much so that when the Ardmore Junior High School building was repurposed to Lower Merion High School, the capstone was preserved and now sits proudly in front of that edifice.

Family members who focus on serving others enrich their families. Each time they find ways to serve, they strengthen family bonds. John Bunyan noted this when he said that one has not lived until they have done something for someone that cannot be repaid.

Hug One Another

A hug is a powerful way to reach out to another with safety and care. We all need the comfort, acceptance, and love that hugs give us. Ann Hood noted that a strong hug is more powerful than a thousand nurturing words.

John's father often reminded him how important it is for an infant to be held. Cuddling a baby is the most important of all hugs. It demonstrates the power of unconditional love. It signals to the baby that they are important; they feel both safe and supported. He believed that you can't touch a child too much; the infant then believes that whether they are in the womb or in their parent's arms, everything is good with the world. Parents that limit their physical contact with their child run the risk that future bonding could be a challenge.

When each family member experiences the power of human touch, they will then embrace hugging as the skill to affirm moments of bonding and bondedness. This physical interaction between family members either reinforces one's bonding with another family member at a family event or confirms that they are already bonded and reflects the joy that the relationship has brought to both of them.

With the advent of Covid, any physical affirmation of bondedness became problematic. Many people rejected physical contact even when they felt it was warranted. Whether pandemic-induced or not, there are those who are just not comfortable with hugging and prefer not to participate. This desire needs to be respected. We believe it best to ask how a given moment should be acknowledged. The responses have ranged from verbal acknowledgment to a handshake to a bump of elbows to a legitimate hug. Acts of celebration are best not forced. What is most important is the mutual recognition of bonding, not the way it is manifested.

John and Sallie hug everyone who wants to be hugged. When John connects with someone, he asks them to celebrate the moment with a hug. What he finds not surprising is that when he asks people if they want to celebrate the connection with a hug, more than half agree to do so. We are wired to express affection for one another through physical contact. We need to keep this tradition going; human touch keeps us human. It is hard to imagine a robot responding to touch as a human would.

It was reported by the press in August 2022, that at a Little League regional playoff game in Waco, Texas, hugging was taken to a new extreme. The player at bat was hit in the head by the opposing pitcher with such force that he fell to the ground. It took some time for him to get up. His coach then examined him and said it was all right for him to stay in the game and advance to first base. The opposing pitcher was obviously distraught and was crying on the mound. The player who was hit then started to advance to the mound to talk to the pitcher. To everyone's surprise, the player embraced the pitcher rather than screaming at him. He said the pitcher needed a hug.

The hug was not only an act of forgiveness but was an act of bonding.

Hug, don't fight. The outcome is better. You will feel that you made a difference.

STEP 4

Explore Family Bonding Strategies

A bond is a close connection between people that occurs as one is touched by an act of kindness, a shared belief or mutual interest is discovered, or there is a shared experience. A bonding moment is the moment when that close connection occurs. After you have mastered the skills that demonstrate respect for others and have adopted the principles that demonstrate love for others, it is time to plan family activities that will facilitate bonding.

Bonding requires family members to be authentic. You can think that you bonded with a family member only to find that he or she presented a false persona. If a family member believes that being right or looking good is more important than being vulnerable, communication becomes a trial rather than an adventure in learning and loving.

Today, we hear discussions about quality time. Spend quality time with your wife, your children, and other family members. Ask yourself, did we spend quality time together?

What is the calculus for rating the time spent? Did you experience something that made you feel joyful, or did you get to know the person better? If you did, you improved the relationship. If you did not, you squandered a great opportunity.

When there is joy in the relationship, celebrate it. Look for what is good in a person and celebrate that discovery. Not every moment generated is a great moment, but when you have a great one, smile, hug them, or say something appreciative.

Well-developed bonding strategies are designed to produce joy that is contagious. Once this contagion gets started, it will spread. When it spreads, it will improve the quality of your family life.

Listed below is a set of strategies to get you thinking. These are the activities that we have found generate bonding moments for our family:

> Remember Birthdays

> Attend/Host Individuals' Events

> Give Meaningful Gifts

> Host Family Parties

> Take Family Trips

> Take Trips for Two

> Attend Sponsored Walks

> ➤ Attend Entertainment Events

> ➤ Explore Genealogy

We will look at each strategy in-depth. This list is not exhaustive, however. Your list should reflect activities that will be an enjoyable backdrop for your family members to spend time together; time that fosters bonding and the important creation of enduring family stories.

Experiment with strategies. Some will work, some will not. Identify what activities produced joy and mutual celebration. If family members call for an event to be repeated, turn it into a family tradition.

We found it increasingly important to keep our strategies "fresh." Changing family dynamics often require the adoption of new bonding strategies. When children become parents and parents become grandparents, new strategies may need to be introduced.

Remember Birthdays

Celebrate each person in the family by remembering their birthday: call, text, or send a card, give a gift, and/or have a party.

When you send a birthday card, select one that best describes your relationship with the individual receiving the card. In this way, you can say why this relationship is important to you.

Handwritten notes are a very personal way to celebrate a relationship. They allow you to say exactly what you want to convey. Texting is also personalized, although some view it as less endearing. You will need to decide your best way to celebrate the birthday.

A gift is a lovely way to recognize someone's importance. Gifts are only limited by your imagination and budget. See "Give Meaningful Gifts" later in this chapter for gift-giving strategies.

Birthday parties are fun and come in many forms. Sometimes, though, to make sure the occasion is celebrated for a family member, you need to be the one to plan and host it. If you are the parent of a child, it is your responsibility to make sure the child feels loved and remembered with a birthday celebration. Spouses want to feel remembered in this way, as well.

Do what you need to do to make the party happen. You may want to host a gathering in a home, congregate at a restaurant, or plot a surprise party.

Although surprise parties can be difficult to plan, they are an extra special thing to do for milestone birthdays. Use these guiding principles. Set a date for the party that is at least two weeks in advance of the family member's actual birthday. You don't want your loved one wondering if you are going to do something for their big occasion. Explain that something is planned. Tall tales are not only permissible for purposes of surprising a loved one, but are mandatory. Reinforce your story with follow-up phone calls and emails. Invite family members well in advance of the planned date to ensure that many attend. Then enjoy the fun. It is important to note that some family members would not feel comfortable being the focus of a surprise party. You need to assess each case.

Remembering birthdays is a great way to demonstrate how important an individual is to a family's life and well-being.

Attend/Host Individuals' Events

Besides birthdays, family members have school plays, sporting events, graduations, recitals, and more. Attend as many of these events as you can, as it will help build a Celebrating Family. If you are attending a child's event, ask how they felt being part of the event and share your impressions of the experience. Mention how much you enjoyed being there.

Depending on your relationship with the individual, you might need to host and/or be on the planning committee for wedding showers, bachelor parties, weddings, baby showers, anniversary parties, and funerals. You need to rise to the occasion. The effort you make will come back many times in family closeness.

See Steps 6 and 7 for honing your event-planning skills.

Give Meaningful Gifts

Select gifts to celebrate what a person means to you; the bond you have together. Gifts don't need to be large to say that you are special.

You can select meaningful gifts in many ways. Ask what would be most special on their wish list. Think about what the person is about and give a gift that would make their socks go up and down. Purchase or make gifts that memorialize moments of bonding.

What is far more important than the monetary value of the gift is the relationship it is meant to celebrate. Gifts are a great way to tell the person receiving them that you connected in a special manner. Both the giver and the receiver see the gift as symbolic of that bond.

Host Family Parties

There is nothing like a big family reunion to foster bonding. If your extended family is too large and you can't invite everyone to every party, plan a big gathering once a year. Then host get-togethers that focus on smaller family groups.

It is particularly important that family members are respectful of one another and treat others how they want to be treated. This will make the event environment feel safe, put people at ease, and allow for fun and laughter to occur. Fun and laughter lead to animated conversations and a meaningful sharing of experiences. This party environment encourages members to speak from the heart.

We have an annual family Christmas party and invite the entire clan. Two meals are served, there is time to share what happened over the year as a group, and we sing Christmas carols. Another family member hosts a July pool party or a day at the beach. This summer party features food, volleyball, and lots of conversation with our feet in the water. If no one has a home large enough to accommodate the entire group, use a beach or a local park.

You will find that having fun together, while critical to bonding, needs to be coupled with a time for reflection when each person acknowledges the importance of the moment. To plan and host a great family party, follow the methods outlined in Steps 6 and 7 of this book. Master these skills and protocols to plan and host family parties of all sizes.

Take Family Trips

Travel with your family. Long trips will work, but short trips will work, too. Exploring provides powerful bonding experiences. Some people feel that they develop a new soul when they tour a new state or country for the first time. Traveling to a new destination with your family will build shared memories and enhance closeness.

There are many types of family trips. Some families simply want to travel to visit with other family members or plan a trip that includes a stop to see extended family. Some enjoy camping. Others enjoy RV trips. Your family may want to focus on golf, skiing, tennis, being on a beach, or hiking in the mountains. Some like to explore a city and go to museums and the theater.

No matter what your interest, there are many ways to plan your trips. Some are inclined to get out a map and plot their own course. Some save their credit card points and points acquired during business travel to purchase flights with stays at big hotel chains including Marriot, Hilton, and others. There are those who enjoy Airbnb, Vrbo, and HomeAway. These organizations list homes of all sizes that are available to rent for vacations for the number of days you desire.

If you own a timeshare, you have weeks that you can use at your home resort or can trade through organizations like Resort Condominiums International. RCI will find a family to use your week and will help you find an exciting location for your family to visit.

Road Scholar can be an exciting option for those who like to study in depth the location they travel to. This organization has a catalogue of courses for trips all over the globe, all focused on those who want to learn. The courses are designed for many categories of learners, including grandparents with grandchildren, those who wish to have an active vacation, and those who prefer less exercise. Tauck Tours and Viking Tours provide higher-end travel with tour guides.

Some families enjoy cruises because a lot of the work is handled for you. The captain does the navigating, and you don't have to pack and unpack at every port of call. Cruises offer a wide variety of cuisines, exercise options, entertainment, and field trips.

You can decide what type of trip suits your family. You can even try many different kinds of trips until you find the one that resonates with the most people. The important thing is to spend time together with an attitude that encourages bonding.

Take Trips for Two

Spend focused time alone with a family member. Trips for two include the range of a honeymoon with your spouse to a yogurt date with your daughter and everything in between. Whether the trips are spontaneous or planned, remove all distractions so that you have time for uninterrupted conversation.

Destinations that are new to both people create a bond of mutual discovery. Perhaps there is an exhibit at the local museum that you both would like to see. Maybe the two of you are interested in a movie that was just released. New doesn't have to mean a big expensive trip. Exploring together is what is extra special and builds lasting memories. If you are looking for destination ideas, see the Take Family Trips chapter for travel suggestions and planning tools. Remember that being together is more important than having a new place to go. You can walk the dog, go to the library, go shopping, or play miniature golf; whatever would be fun for the two of you. Select activities that spur conversation, not limit it.

You might want to try getting in the car for a day trip with only a general destination in mind. Make decisions as you go. Find a new place to walk on a beach. Find a new place for lunch using Yelp or TripAdvisor or ask someone on the street for a recommendation. Local people are happy to share their favorites.

Many years ago, we realized that those moments we spent together in the car were extremely productive from an organizational standpoint. The focused time permitted us to quickly identify marital objectives and make progress on family projects. Use the day trip to an unknown destination as a chance to make important decisions and then have some fun when you arrive.

Couples with young children must plan carefully to have the time they need together. Find trusted babysitters by getting recommendations from friends. Perhaps nearby relatives would enjoy spending time with your children. YMCAs, churches, and other organizations have Kids Nite Out programs. The internet will help you find what is in your area and will specify the age of children they cater to. If possible, plan a trip during the school day or ask other parents to take your children for a period of time with an agreement to reciprocate. Identify what strategies work for you.

Trips for two provide one-on-one time over a shared experience that is mutually interesting. The destination is less important than the journey, the purpose of which is to communicate and have fun. You are only limited by your imagination to create these bonding opportunities.

Attend Sponsored Walks

Every family has been touched by disease and its heartbreak. Attending sponsored walks to raise money in the name of a family member who has suffered is very bonding.

Find a medical cause that your family will embrace. Then walk to raise money for its cure. Visit the website of the organization sponsoring the events for your cause.

The first time you and other family members walk, you will learn how the event is run. If you enjoy the experience and wish to do it again, form a team to raise money for the cause. Pick a name that honors those family members who suffered with the disease. Have special t-shirts made. It is not the amount of money you raise that is important, it is about being together to support a common goal. Make sure to have a meal afterwards to celebrate the event. This will cement the bonding process and make the event that much more meaningful.

Attend Entertainment Events

Attend entertainment events with a group of family members with time planned to catch up afterward. Going to the event and then having a meal together to relive the highlights produces great bonding moments. This strategy works best when the event is enjoyable and there is much to talk about.

If you have a group of family members who would like to go to the theater, look for interesting plays that your group will enjoy. Colleges with theater departments provide affordable quality entertainment. Look also to high school offerings. Professional theater groups are a possibility but come with a higher price tag. Research what is available nearby. Select an offering that will prompt active theater dialogue, provocative discussions, possible bonding moments, and put it on your calendar. Share the costs.

If you have family members who enjoy viewing sporting events, attending them as a group also offers opportunities for bonding. Select offerings from local high schools, colleges, minor leagues, and professional teams. The group can also convene at someone's home to watch games. It is always more fun if your team wins, but no matter who wins, great camaraderie is built discussing players, teams, plays, and past games.

Your family may have different entertainment preferences; perhaps you like the ballet, orchestra, pop concerts, or jazz. Select events that will generate active sharing of thoughts, observations, and joy. Share a meal together afterward.

Explore Genealogy

Getting to know your family genealogy will change you in untold ways. When you embark on the journey to 'meet' your ancestors, you will gain the feeling of being connected to something greater than yourself.

Compile your family tree. Gather information from the eldest living members. Old marriage certificates, birth certificates, baptismal certificates, deeds, death certificates, and family Bibles can provide much information. Use ancestry.com or similar sites to help you enter and maintain your family tree. They will also provide the names and information of additional people who might be part of your genealogy.

Cemeteries and small-town historians are filled with leads for families that wish to learn about their family trees. When practical, visit locations where family members lived.

Family members love to learn about their heritage and see where they came from.

Use country-specific ancestry sites, such as German-ancestry.com or Frenchancestry.com and/or whatever is appropriate for your family's genealogy. When you locate the address of a relative who lived in another country, locate the town on a map. Show your children where their relatives came from. Ask at the library for books about immigrants who came to your country from this region. Read about their stories. Were they persecuted and left seeking religious freedom? Was there a famine that sent them looking for a better place to live? Was there a war? Some towns provide virtual tours. Books provide pictures. Traveling to these places can be very rewarding and very bonding. You will go through many unique bonding experiences searching for the homes and towns of those who elected to relocate in search of a new life and the homes of those who didn't leave their country. If you haven't been able to locate a relative with an address but you are clear which country they were from, visit the country with your family or read about it.

Exploring genealogy can be an important source of memorable bonding moments that enrich your family's heritage.

STEP 5

Review Bonding Strategies that Work for You

Think about the great bonding moments you have already experienced. What facilitated them? What were the circumstances? Can they be revisited? What has not worked for you? Which bonding strategies that we mentioned in Step 4 would you like to try?

We have described many of our special bonding moments to get you thinking about the magic you can produce. The event bonding moments chronicled in this section confirm our belief that bonding moments do not happen by chance, but by careful planning of events. We hope these stories will inspire you.

Birthday Moments

Tom is John's youngest brother. To celebrate Tom's seventieth birthday, Sallie and John and his brothers and their wives gathered for lunch at a restaurant in the Hershey Hotel. In advance of the day, we thought about what we could do to celebrate Tom. We each brought our favorite "brother" quotes and, going around the table one by one, presented them to Tom. We had t-shirts made for everyone that said "Brant Beach" on the front, a reference to the New Jersey town where we enjoyed the surf and sun together on a Sunday every August. On the back was written "Anna's Allies." Anna was the name of John's mother. Her relatives were her allies when they walked to raise money for ALS. In addition, we each gave Tom a birthday card with a message of appreciation. Tom felt especially loved that day.

Surprise Party Moments

We hosted a surprise party for John's brother Dave's seventieth birthday. Dave is the toughest person to surprise, but we set out to do just that. We had to find a way to get him to our house without his suspecting what was up. When we were in Asbury Park for a day trip, we called Dave to say we wanted to take him and his wife to dinner for his approaching decade birthday and wanted to talk about possible restaurants that he might enjoy. We invited friends and family to our home and plotted a big surprise.

When the day of our "trip" to Asbury Park arrived, Sallie asked Dave and his wife to come to our house so that we could make the trip together. Strangely, the Philadelphia Inquirer printed a major spread advertising Asbury Park that day as a great place to visit. We took that to be a good omen.

Our living room was filled with the large group that had gathered with quiet anticipation. John sat alone at the kitchen table as he always did when expecting Dave. Dave arrived, opened the door, and was greeted by everyone saying Happy Birthday. "You got me!" he responded.

He was thrilled. It was great to celebrate someone who has done so much for our family.

Individual Members' Event Moments

Baptism Moments

Our son, John, and his wife, Carolin, returned to the United States for the baptism of their son, Oliver David, who was named after Uncle Dave. The ceremony took place in our home. Carolin's family in Germany joined us via Zoom. John's siblings and cousins made long trips to be with them, as did Sallie's brother and his wife. John's sister, Julie, and her husband, Brad, as the godparents, were part of the ceremony.

Carolin and John chose the music, "The Holy City," which was sung spiritedly as a Raezer Fight Song with Sallie playing the piano.

Afterward, there was a sumptuous buffet. Carolin prepared her authentic German potato salad. Son John manned the grill and afterward conducted a tasting event where he shared several beers from the brewery he founded.

Everyone loved being together to share the occasion, celebrating with familiar songs, great food, and a flight of beer.

Sporting Event Moments

Sallie's dad, Larry, grew up playing tennis in California. He was captain of the tennis team for his college. You can imagine his excitement when his granddaughter, Julie, started playing serious tennis. He and Sallie's mom, Peg, became regulars at Julie's high school and United States Tennis Association tournaments. It was not unusual for them to appear at matches six hours from their home on Long Island. If they couldn't be courtside, they always called in for results. They had found joy in following Julie's tennis matches and in so doing, became a reliable presence in her life.

Julie's Lower Merion High School Varsity tennis team went to the state finals each of the four years that Julie played. Family members congregated first in Altoona and later in Hershey to watch Julie and her teammates play. Going into the fourth attempt at clinching the state title, Julie's team had a more serious attitude than ever before. They had lost three years in a row and were extra hungry for a victory. Under captain Julie Raezer they practiced extra hard all season, thought about eating well, and went to bed early the night before the big event. The Lower Merion team did not lose one set in the finals. They won the state championship with a decisive win. It was so exciting! Grandma Peg was thrilled to be there. Julie felt so supported by her family.

Funeral Moments

Sallie's cousin Charlyn and her husband, Rob, drove from Dandridge, Tennessee, to be at Julie and Brad's wedding.

They stayed in our home, as did our son, John, and his wife, Carolin, who arrived from Germany for the occasion. It was the last time that they would all spend time with Rob, who later died of cancer.

The whole family loved Rob. Extra precious are the memories of his big smile and quick wit, and of course, the way he went out of his way to make everyone a delicious scrapple and pancake breakfast.

The weekend celebration of life events that Sallie, John, and Julie attended in Tennessee was as special as Rob was. Rob was one of eight children. Present were Rob's ninety-two-year-old mom, his seven siblings, and their families. The love was palpable. To them, Rob's loss was unthinkable.

The service reflected all the love. The choir sang Rob's favorite hymns. The entire ministry staff, as well as family members and friends, shared warm memories of a person who loved people, who was a cohesive force of love that sought ways to help, and who was intentional in his attempts to nurture others. All told of a person who worked incredibly hard, lived a life of service that glorified God, and whose infectious smile would not be forgotten.

He was gone too soon. What wonderful family bonds he built.

Gift Moments

When John graduated from college, his father gave him a gold belt buckle. On that buckle were two engraved laurel leaves, symbolic of his graduating with high honors. To celebrate their relationship, John's father had the same jeweler create a set of cuff links engraved with those same laurel leaves for himself. Although his father never formally expressed his love for John, years later John realized that with that gift, he had. This was their greatest moment of bonding, for which John was eternally grateful.

For Sallie's fiftieth birthday, John, unbeknownst to Sallie, took a reel of tape that had her Bucknell University senior recital on it to a company that would transfer it to CD format. On the way to a surprise party for Sallie, John started playing the CD. Sallie recognized quickly that it was a recording of her playing the piano. She was so surprised and thought it was a gift that was beyond special.

When Julie had her first brain surgery, Sallie's sister sent Sallie and Julie silver bracelets. Her note explained that she and her daughter would wear the same bracelets until Julie had fully recovered from her brain tumor and suggested that we do the same. Sallie and Julie were so touched by this gift.

When Julie's older siblings, Jimmy, Kara, and Laurie, heard that Julie was to undergo a third brain surgery, they decided they would have a Peloton bike sent to her house. They wanted to have something special for her to look forward to after her hospital stay. It turned out to be a great gift. There is a community of users and Julie gets to see how much her sister, Laurie, exercises and vice versa. There is a schedule of classes that Julie regularly enjoys, including time for meditation. Sallie gave our son, John, her grandmother's diamond to use for the engagement ring that he gave to Carolin. Sallie's generous gift forever bonds Carolin to our family, as well as her family to ours.

The night before John and Carolin's wedding, Carolin's family hosted a traditional German party called a Polterabend. It is their custom to have their guests break porcelain to bring luck to the couple's marriage. Quite a mess of broken glass is made, as you can imagine. The bride and groom are expected to clean it up together as their first shared marital responsibility. When John and Carolin were not looking, Sallie filled a bag with many of the beautiful broken glass pieces. She then had an artist craft a frame from the fragments. The Polterabend frame now holds their wedding picture in celebration of their marriage.

Each of these gift moments is touching in its deep meaning and enduring emotional impact. The giver and the receiver cherish a lasting bond.

Family Party Moments

John's brother, Tom, and his family established our second family event, a July pool party at his home. They served a buffet lunch, to which everybody contributed a dish or drink.

At the first such event, time was allotted for a water volleyball game, which quickly became a tradition. What started out with a random pairing of teams soon gave way to the battle of the ages. It was the older people (which happened to include John and his two brothers) in the shallow end of the pool versus the younger people. When they couldn't win with the shallow-end advantage, John's brother, Dave, started changing the rules. Dave made himself the referee and made all the calls, including bad ones, which prompted a lot of debate and bantering. Dave also claimed players from the deep end that were playing well. His mission was simple: position the opposition in such a way as to ensure the older guys a victory. Family members kept the game moments lively by constantly kidding and splashing one another. Julie's Brad just observed his first year and was appalled. After that, he became a regular and joined in on the fun. When Dave saw how well Brad played, he moved Brad to the shallow end. The old guys' team continued to try to win through scoring chicanery, lots of overruling, and competitive double talk. It was a fun bonding event!

Family Trip Moments

Family trips have long been important to us, and we worked hard to make them happen over the years. We traded our timeshare floating weeks to take John and Julie to a new state every summer when they were young. The family visited traditional tourist sites, including the Grand Canyon, Lake Tahoe, and the coast of Maine, but it was the lesser-known locations that we have talked about the most. Top of that list were the visits to Frank Lloyd Wright's homes, Taliesin, in Spring Green, Wisconsin, and Taliesin West in Phoenix, Arizona; Mount Lemon in Tucson; Arches National Park in Utah; Charleston, South Carolina; Savannah, Georgia; and

Quebec City. Our most symbolic bonding activity occurred at the four corners monument where the four of us, each standing in a different state, joined hands as a symbol of family and geographical unity.

One year, Sallie suggested that we take the whole family, twenty of us, to Smugglers Notch for a week of summer activities. She traded timeshare winter ski weeks for summer weeks and provided condos for Jimmy, Kara, and Laurie and their families. Everybody set aside time to be there together.

Each family was assigned an evening to prepare dinner for everyone. When it was our turn, son John and his future wife, Carolin, suggested that we have a raclette dinner. A raclette grill allows groups to simulate the cooking of the traditional meal prepared by Swiss shepherds over a campfire in the Alps. Everyone has their own "shovel" to place under the heat to melt raclette cheese on vegetables. On top of the grill, shrimp, meat, and pineapple are cooked to perfection. It is unlikely that the shepherds used shrimp and pineapple, but it sure is good. Using a common grill to cook our food produced smiles all around, lots of lively conversation, and much multigenerational bonding.

Smuggler's Notch has bungee jumping, and our family decided to get in on the act. The highlight of bungee jumping for the younger generation was Sallie's back flip. One grandson was so impressed. He told Sallie that this was an incredible accomplishment for a woman of her age.

Sallie, John, and Julie had their own little bonding event. Each rented a Segway, and with the help of a guide, navigated the lower regions of one of the ski mountains. The adventure ended with the guide taking a picture of the three of them, which Julie then texted to the entire family.

One afternoon, we all decided to play disc golf, a game in which each player throws Frisbee-style discs at poles with chain baskets hoping to drop the disc in the basket. It incited moments of laughter and fun. John was relieved at the fifth hole that we had to leave the course to seek shelter from a very active thunderstorm. This produced a great bonding experience for two reasons: the first was obvious, the fun of navigating the course together; the second less obvious, joining together to wait through a violent thunderstorm.

Later in the trip, John and a grandson competed as a team doing some traditional camping games. At the end, they were tied with another team. The final challenge was to toss an egg between them at greater and greater distances. They did so successfully several times. This was not enough. The other team simply had better tosses and better hands. John learned that it was not whether they won or lost, but the fact that they competed together, that made the difference. This created a special bond between Granddad and grandson.

As part of the trip to Smuggler's Notch, the family spent a whole afternoon on a raft in the reservoir at the base of Madonna Mountain. Son John jumped hard onto one end of the rubber raft, catapulting a child at the other end of the raft high into the air and then down into the water.

This was a giant hit among all his young nephews. This activity was so well received that John spent the rest of the day captaining the raft. A funny aftermath of the trip to the reservoir occurred the next day. We inquired at the front desk about the availability of the raft. To our surprise, we were told that overnight the raft had sunk to the bottom of the reservoir. Did we wear it out?

We had such a great time at Smuggs that five years later, there was a family call to do it again.

Trips for Two Moments

As a couple, we are well known for our day trips. Friends jokingly comment that our being in the car together is more important than where we are going. It's true, we are on a sharing journey rather than a traveling one. On one occasion, we selected a restaurant in Strathmere, New Jersey, that was new to us and ate dandelion ravioli for the first time. What a joy! During a trip to Cape May, New Jersey, we particularly enjoyed the sunset pyrotechnics. The setting of the sun caused an explosion of yellows, reds, and oranges. Spectacular!

With Sallie's arms around John's waist, we visited every parish in Bermuda on a motorbike. On one ride, we passed the art gallery and studio of Alfred Birdsey, an artist who was well-known for his watercolors of Bermuda scenes. We decided to go in. Sallie was looking through the paintings and was not finding what she wanted. Suddenly a gentleman tapped her on the shoulder asking what she was looking for. She told him she wanted a picture of the city of Hamilton. He replied that she should follow him to his studio. He would paint a picture of Hamilton for her. Sallie quickly understood that this was Alfred Birdsey himself. John followed them to the studio. It was fascinating to see the artist take a white candle and rub it on certain places on the empty canvas. Then he filled his brush with one color at a time and put paint to canvas. He seemed to know where the brush strokes should go. When he had applied a light blue, a dark blue, yellow, and orange, he picked up an ink pen and added lines to the canvas, again seeming to already know where they went. The picture was complete, and Sallie was thrilled. He then asked John about his interests. John spoke about his love of sailing. Mr. Birdsey followed the same steps to produce a stunning harbor scene filled with sailboats for John. Many decades later these pictures invoke special memories.

Sallie had Mount Rushmore on her bucket list. When we attended a wedding in driving distance of South Dakota, we decided it was time to go. The drive there was more stressful than we expected. Our phones put out an alarm for a tornado. The message was to find shelter immediately. There was one big problem; there was no shelter in sight for miles and the tornado was approaching. We stopped at a gas station and were told to lie down in a ditch and hope not to drown. Can you imagine? We elected to keep driving and very, very luckily avoided the tornado. Harrowing but bonding! The Fourth of July fireworks at Mount Rushmore were fabulous! We loved exploring South Dakota. Was it worth the tornado drive for those moments? YES!

Over the years, the two of us have shared some funny travel culinary moments. On our honeymoon to Norway, we took a two-week trip on a boat that delivered mail to all the ports going up and down the coast. On the mail boat we had a delicious meal of what we thought was fried oyster. When we asked for seconds, we were told it was cod tongue, which came as a bit of a shock. In Bergen, Norway, a waitress offered us a beer steak. Sallie asked if that was a steak marinated in beer. The answer was no, no, no, it is a grizzly 'beer' steak. In a restaurant in Brig, Switzerland, we tried to order from a hunter's menu. Not knowing what chamois meant, we requested a French-English translation dictionary. The dictionary didn't help. The English translation was chamois, the same word. It wasn't until we arrived home that we found we had eaten mountain goat. In Talloires, France, we were asked to leave a restaurant because John insisted on having his coffee before his fromage. We bonded over being clueless Americans.

There is one day trip that we remember as our worst day ever. We visited Atlantic City. We began gambling at one of the casinos and lost our stake. Then we walked the boardwalk and found a store to buy ice cream cones. As we left the store, Sallie turned toward the wind and at that moment the scoop of ice cream in her cone became a scoop of ice cream on our faces and in our hair. We got in the car at the parking lot, and someone yelled out that our fuel line had been cut and that gasoline was pouring out. We stopped at a nearby White Castle to call AAA for roadside service. After completing the call, John noticed a cop talking to Sallie. Instead of offering to help, he was asking Sallie to join him gambling. Sallie asked him to move on. AAA arrived after a very long wait. In preparing to tow the car to a nearby station, AAA ripped the bumper off our car. The second attempt was successful, and the car was towed to a nearby station where the gas line was repaired. On the way home, it rained so hard that we had to park under a bridge to weather the onslaught. We smiled at each other and laughed. The day was so bad, we could not have made it up. Bonding can also happen when things go terribly wrong if you bring along a positive attitude.

On each of our trips we had set aside time to be together. We could not have planned the special things that occurred when we did. Years later those special things are what we talk about. They are what bonds us.

Sponsored Walk Moments

The first sponsored walk we attended was in Ocean City, New Jersey. We joined the fight against ALS, commonly called Lou Gehrig's disease, in 2012, to honor John's mother. After a couple of walks, we formed our own team, Anna's Allies. Our daughter, Julie, was the first to join our team. Other family members joined the following year. After each walk, the team shared a meal, celebrating both John's mother, Anna, and a day well spent. The team bonded in its efforts to help eradicate this terrible disease.

In April of 2016, Julie asked family members to join her for a Brain Tumor walk in Asbury Park, New Jersey. The walk was the first for this venue. It brought several younger people together to share their fight against brain cancer and listen to the band, The Poorly Educated. It poured rain the whole morning, but that did not deter us from walking. All of us were there to celebrate Julie's courageous fight against one of the toughest forms of cancer.

The next year, Julie formed PSU Brain Buddies with another brain tumor survivor named Charlie, who she had met in the radiation waiting room at Jefferson Hospital in Philadelphia. The two became fast friends as they were on the same radiation treatment schedule every morning for three weeks. Julie was a graduate of Penn State and Charlie was a Penn State professor. They both had Penn State T-shirts on. Members of both families signed up to walk for their team and raised money to help find a cure for brain cancer.

Since then, our family members and Charlie's family members have been regulars at the Asbury Park walk. A celebratory lunch at Porta Restaurant has become the team's "after the walk" tradition. Many of us wear National Brain Tumor Society bracelets in support of Julie and Charlie.

Genealogy Exploration Moments

Carolin was the force behind bonding moments through genealogy. Using Ancestry.de, Carolin, who is German, was able to determine that Sallie's grandmother, Bertha Haus, was from the very small town of Diersheim in western

Germany. Carolin contacted the historical society there and asked about Bertha Haus. The town historian was able to set up a visit with a ninety-three-year-old relative, Hans Haus. He was still living in the original family home that had been partially damaged by a bomb in World War II and then restored.

We drove to Diersheim to meet Hans. Carolin translated. There was a moment of discovery as Hans was showing us pictures of his family when Sallie pointed out that she had some of the same family pictures in her albums at home. This brought tears to the eyes of everyone present in an unexpected moment of bonding. Hans filled in where Sallie had no knowledge of the family tree.

The Diersheim historian gave us a tour of the village museum. We tried on period hats that the women wore to church. They were four feet wide and would have blocked the view of anyone sitting behind them. The hats would also have hit anyone sitting next to them in the face. We laughed about this strange custom and wondered what our relatives were thinking.

The Raezer (originally Roeser) genealogy pointed to Beddelhausen, Germany, as the origin of John's father's family. Carolin called the town historian and identified the church where the Roesers had worshipped. When the group visited there, we saw Johannes Roeser's name etched on the back of a pew and dated 1625. We later visited with a town historian who was writing a book about the emigration of four thousand Anabaptists to Pennsylvania in the early

1700s. They left as Anabaptists were being beheaded in the nearby town of Muenster.

Carolin mentioned that with her marriage to our son John, our family had come full circle. All families traced were not only German, but also to the precise regions of Germany from which they emigrated. We found that this discovery was bonding not only for our family but bonding to Carolin's family, as well.

Master Event-Planning Skills

You must get people spending time together to build family unity. We have found that the work it takes to make family events meaningful is more than rewarded by the goodwill and sense of belonging they create.

Simply getting together, though, is not enough. The following skills will guide you to plan an event that encourages family participation and interaction:

> ➢ Learn to Set a Date and Send Invitations

> ➢ Learn to Prepare and Purchase Delicious Food

> ➢ Learn to Select Engaging Music

> ➢ Learn to Select Games

> ➢ Learn to Conduct Circle Time

> ➢ Learn to Toast

Learn to Set a Date and Send Invitations

It can be tricky finding a time when everyone is available for your party. You will want to set a date when all or most of your family members can come. You want to make sure everyone feels wanted.

If you have a large family and do not know their schedules, an app called Doodle will simplify the job for you. Doodle allows you to select several possible dates and collects feedback about those dates from the people on your guest list. It will show you which date works for the most people. You can contact the others to see what their issues are and open up the conversation. Some people will be able to rearrange plans, others not. We have used Doodle quite successfully to find dates for our events.

For an annual party, you may find that you don't need to use Doodle. Perhaps it has already given you the understanding you need about your family's schedules. Our extended family knows that our Christmas party will be held the second Saturday before Christmas because it works for most people. We just check the calendar each year to find out what that date is.

Once you have a date, send invitations. Use Evite or a similar site. Evite allows you to select an appropriate invitation format and enter the party particulars: host, location, date, and starting time. It also does the work to manage the RSVPs.

Learn to Prepare and Purchase Delicious Food

Critical to creating family bonds is the use of great food, as it is the best way of bringing people together. The breaking of bread and the sharing of wine were biblical catalysts for group discourse and understanding. Savoring a meal together fosters intimacy and promotes unscripted dialogue that allows individuals to get to know one another.

What is the definition of great food? It is food that reflects the tastes and needs of those attending. It is food that is sensitive to allergies and dislikes. For those who gather often, it provides something new and interesting. Most importantly, it is delicious.

What is tasty and a special treat to one might not be tolerated by the next. You must be aware of those who avoid certain food categories or have allergies so that you can plan appropriate menus. We have found that reviewing the proposed menu with those who will be with us is good practice. This way we won't be serving escargot to someone who would find it intolerable.

Drinks are a separate category that requires consideration. You need to plan appropriate drinks for children. For adults who prefer an alcoholic drink with a meal, there are wine and spirit stores that will suggest pairings of wines to what you will be serving. You need to remember those who don't drink alcohol and have something appropriate for them as well.

A cook must have great recipes. Robert Frost said that there is one thing more exasperating than a person who can cook and won't, and that's a person who can't cook and will. One is only as good as the recipe he or she is about to use. If you think your recipe is not a ten, press on to find a better one. As vendors and their products vary dramatically, you also need to know where to acquire ingredients that work well for your recipe.

Everyone enjoys variety. A wonderful new recipe provides much happiness and gives you a new way to love your family and friends. You can gather ideas for new foods to serve when you enjoy something new in a restaurant or at someone else's table. Share recipes. The internet and cookbooks provide lots of suggestions for preparation, as well.

Sometimes when you have a dinner party, you would like each guest to bring a dish. Rather than requesting specifically a salad or bread or an appetizer, initiate the menu with an entrée or two that will work for everyone, and then ask others to add what they would like to bring to compliment it. People tend to suggest their signature dish, and this will result in very tasty, interesting meals.

On another occasion you might host a "participatory" meal. Fill a giant bowl with noodles and a steaming Pho broth. Encourage guests to customize their bowl of soup with a choice of different toppings. This is fun and will be well received.

Raclette grills also provide a participatory experience. The grill, placed in the middle of the table, allows each guest to cook what they want to eat, customizing their meal of shrimp, beef, and veggies with melted cheese.

Sharing great food nourishes our bodies, lifts our spirits, and bonds our families.

Learn to Select Engaging Music

Plato said that music gives soul to the universe and life to everything. Since we are all touched by music, music can be used to promote family bonding. If properly planned, your family members will experience moments of great joy.

As Sallie's mother thought that music was extremely important, Sallie and her siblings were at their instruments by six o'clock each morning. Sallie is now a piano teacher. Most of her students' parents believe, as her mother did, that the study of music has far-reaching positive life benefits. Shinichi Suzuki, who wrote *Nurtured by Love: The Classic Approach to Talent Education*, said that if a child hears good music and learns to play it himself, he develops sensitivity and discipline. It makes for a beautiful heart.

We have witnessed the impact of music when we attend professional football games. At Philadelphia Eagles games, our seats are surrounded by strangers. We are strangers, though, only until our team scores its first touchdown. Then fans leap to their feet and celebrate by singing "Fly Eagles Fly." There are high fives all around. Team management worked hard to select a song that would promote bonding. They succeeded.

In Sallie's piano teaching, she is often reminded that as much as music is universally loved, the actual music that speaks to each of us can be very different. For that reason, she has her students participate in the selection of the pieces that they want to learn. Sallie plays compositions that they are ready for and looks to see if she gets a thumbs up. She seeks a selection that speaks to their heart. There will be no motivation to practice if they are not thrilled to learn to play that particular piece. With the "right" music there is palpable joy, and she might hear a parent say that he couldn't keep his hands off the piano. With the "wrong" music, the piano won't be touched that week. The same applies to selecting music for an event.

Sallie and John planned a Thanksgiving dinner, inviting not only family members, but also members of their church who had no place to go for a turkey dinner. They compiled a CD of songs about giving thanks and added some that they thought also might be enjoyed. During dinner, John's brother, Dave, asked where they had acquired such great music. He now listens to it on the way to work every day.

Some families have strong traditions of singing together. Sallie's cousins always mention how on Christmas Day at Sallie's parents' home, everyone would gather around the piano to sing Christmas carols. Their favorite song was "The Holy City." Sallie introduced "The Holy City" to the Raezer family, and we have embraced it almost as a fight song. Now all of us together stand for the chorus and raise our right arms to Jerusalem, Jerusalem. It has been heartwarming to have that tradition pass to the next generation.

John hosted a bachelor party at our home a few years back. The "planning committee" of two discussed what music would be near and dear to the groom's heart and put a CD together. It started with "On the Way to Cape May," as the wedding couple spend a lot of time there, included "Bobby's Girl" (the groom was Bob), and "When a Man Loves a Woman" as well. The CD was also played at the bridal shower. This gift of music was a giant hit at both parties.

Sallie's longtime piano teacher, Alexander Fiorillo, always spoke of making the melody sing. What a great metaphor for a life well lived! Whenever possible, include time spent together with a musical message of hope and optimism that leaves you feeling uplifted and bonded. Everyone departs with their souls well nourished.

Learn to Select Games

One of the most important books on non-bonding is Robert Putnam's book *Bowling Alone*. "Putnamites" talk about the decline of communal activities. In this age of cell phones and virtual reality, the focus is on individual rather than group activities or get-togethers. Putnam painstakingly reminds his reader that more and more people are bowling alone. They no longer congregate to play cards, visit the local Knights of Columbus or Italian American clubs, go to a church or a synagogue, or participate in quilting bees and book clubs. While many older citizens continue to get together, younger citizens tend to go it alone.

Roald Dahl extolled the importance of fun when he said that even the wisest of people cherish time for a little bit of shared nonsense. How do you select playful activities? Some games, like well-chosen food and music, encourage bonding moments. Use games in as many events as possible, concentrating on those that encourage team cooperation and creativity.

One of our favorites is Apples to Apples, which is played with four to ten people. Rated for ages twelve and up, it is fun for those who enjoy a game that fosters creative and strange pairings of words that will provoke lots of laughter. Surprising and outrageous matches produce a lot of conversation and many bonding moments.

Qwirkle is another popular game for two to four players or up to four teams with two players each. It is rated for ages six and up. It is all about matching colors and shapes in a way that scores the most points. If someone in the group is new to the game, teach the rules while playing with open hands for everyone to see. It is fun to discuss the possible moves.

The game of Klask, played in Denmark's pubs, is a small table-top version of ice hockey for two players. The competitors go head-to-head on a wooden surface using steering magnets to drive a ball into the opponent's goal. It takes a short time to play and requires quick thinking and dexterity to win. It is a favorite in our family with adults and children alike. You can have one game of it going with everyone watching and waiting to de-throne the victor, or you can have two games going and have even more fun.

Cornhole is a fun game where you try to throw bags filled with corn or resin pellets into the hole on a tilted platform. It is played one on one or in teams of two, three, or four people. The first team to score twenty-one wins. The standard court has a platform at each end twenty-seven feet apart. The large distance makes it a good outdoor game. Smaller platforms can be purchased for young children and can be placed at much shorter distances. Spectators will clap when bags drop in the hole and will ooh and ahh when there is a close try.

Marble runs are engaging and intriguing to both children and adults. They can provide extended fun and entertainment for groups of all ages.

You will find that participatory games enhance family events. Be on the lookout for new games that will engage your family members and provide moments of togetherness.

Learn to Conduct Circle Time

What is Circle Time? James O'Dea said that whenever it is possible, create a circle where people can safely share deep experiences. He said that in so doing you demonstrate reverence for the truth of another's experience. In our family, we separate Circle Time from other activities because we have found from a bonding standpoint that it is the most effective activity of all.

Everyone assembles in our family room sitting and standing roughly in a circle. John's brother David guides the process. Going around the room, he asks each person to speak to where they have been and where they are going and what this moment together means to them. Each member re-bonds himself or herself to the group by sharing from the heart. If someone rambles too much, Uncle David will stop them by utilizing his infamous hook.

While Circle Time rules are not extensive, they are important.

> Rule 1: New attendees may elect to observe for as many times as they need to feel comfortable.

> Rule 2: Children under seven are welcome to listen unless they prefer to participate.

> Rule 3: Keep it pithy, otherwise the hook.

After each member speaks, their contribution is acknowledged. It is important that each member feel supported and appreciated.

All kinds of family news is shared during this time: engagements, babies on the way, and more. Circle Time has meant so much to our family that we recommend that you schedule it at an event at least once a year.

We have included, via Zoom, those members who live too far away to attend. Our son, John, and his family who live in Germany were present and participated in Circle Time during our last Christmas party. Since we assign a time for Circle Time to begin, Zoom connections are not difficult to plan.

Learn to Toast

Toasting offers its giver the opportunity to present a verbal message of celebration. It may be a happy birthday message or a message pointing out an area of appreciation. The toaster confirms by clicking the glass of the person honored, and everyone at the table joins in with a round of clicks and "hear, hear" in agreement. It is very affirming to be toasted and is very bonding.

Many of you are shy and lack the confidence to give a toast. If you would like to know more about toasting, and are serious about improving your public speaking skills, there are organizations like Toastmasters International and Dale Carnegie that have offerings that will help you with this.

STEP 7

Establish an Annual Family Party Event

I f your family does not get together for an annual event, it is time to start planning one now that you have mastered the skills in Step 6. In this chapter, we will guide you through how to put these skills to work to create a successful event.

If your family already has an annual event in place and you would like to turn it into a great bonding experience, this chapter will make suggestions that will help you do so.

In either case, you will need to decide on the type of event you want to hold. Is it a December holiday party, a backyard barbecue, a pool party, or a destination location? When this is decided, determine the venue and set a date. Then do the following:

➤ Select Activities

➤ Plan the Schedule

➤ Plan the Menu

> ➢ Plan the Music

> ➢ Share the Work

> ➢ Share the Costs

Select Activities

Choose group activities that encourage bonding. We recommend including Circle Time in the day's activities, as it provides a great way to build close family connections.

The type of event, time of year, and interests, traditions, and locations of family members will generally dictate appropriate activities. If the event is a December holiday party, perhaps a carol sing is appropriate; if the event is a pool party, water volleyball may be of interest. The objective: have fun and play together. Bond!

Make sure there is a plan to keep young children safe and engaged when the adult activities are not appropriate for them.

Plan the Schedule

Estimate the time required for each activity and each meal and build a schedule that will make it all fit. Remember to leave a block of time at the beginning for everyone to arrive.

Event timetables tend to slip if not managed well. Assign a responsible person to keep an eye on the clock and keep the event moving along. You don't want to be forced to eliminate an activity you were looking forward to because you ran out of time.

Families with young children usually prefer that a party start early in the day so that they can leave at a reasonable time to get everyone to bed. Keep this in mind when setting your schedule. Our annual Christmas party starts at noon and ends at about 7 p.m. Many of our relatives drive a long way, so we emphasize a lot of visiting and don't want anyone to leave hungry. Below is the order of activities for our event:

> Meet and Greet with Drinks and Hors d'oeuvres

> Light Lunch

> Visiting

> Circle Time

> Visiting

> Dinner

> Carol Sing

> Dessert

> Good-byes

Make sure there is sufficient time for each activity so that your guests don't feel rushed.

Plan the Menu

The event menu needs to be carefully planned. The time of day will dictate if you are planning brunch, lunch, drinks and hors d'oeuvres, dinner, or just desserts.

Next, determine the number of adults and children attending. Put together a menu that will appeal to both children and adults.

If the group is small, you can ask for individual likes and dislikes. If the group is large, you need to provide enough variety to satiate the hunger of those who wish to eat healthily, those who are gluten sensitive, and those who are vegetarians. Everybody needs to find something they can eat and enjoy.

Your menu can include a mix of foods prepared at home, purchased from buying clubs, restaurant take-out, and catered specialties. The items you prepare at home will help you to stay within your budget, as will buying club products that typically come in large quantities. Take-out and catered items save preparation time but can be expensive. It is important to strike a proper balance between cost and effort.

It is risky to try new recipes on company. It is also risky to serve purchased food that you haven't tried. Sample food that you are considering from take-out ahead of time. Caterers will also give you a chance to taste test. It needs to be both delicious and affordable.

Plan the Music

Prepare a song playlist that you think your guests will enjoy. Use it as background music to create a festive and welcoming party environment when your guests arrive. If you follow their arrival with drinks and hors d'oeuvres, you may wish to continue the musical backdrop, ensuring that it is not too loud to converse.

When we first hosted a family Christmas party, we included a time for singing carols. We requested that our guests bring Christmas music so that everyone had a copy to sing from. It was a frustrating exercise, though, as everyone sang from different arrangements with different lyrics. The next year we eliminated the chaos by creating a book of lyrics that matched the arrangements that Sallie played and then printed enough copies for everyone to use.

Create your own book of lyrics. If you have a musician in the family, ask him or her to select arrangements and lyrics that are familiar to everyone. If you do not have a musician in the crowd, you can sing a cappella. Look online to find lyrics that you are familiar with. Type the lyrics to each song. Print out copies. Add songs as requested. Enjoy the bonding that singing together engenders.

Share the Work

When planning an event, sharing the workload is extremely important. You can't do it all alone. The party works if family members divide the tasks. Not only does sharing lighten the burden, but everyone feels great about contributing to achieve a mutual goal.

There are many ways to divide the tasks. For example, assign one or more persons to decorate the venue. Assign another to send invitations and track RSVPs. Another can plan the menu and place orders for food. Ask someone to pick up food orders and enlist others to prepare food. Another can organize the music. Others can stay to clean up afterwards. The sharing of work creates many bonding opportunities and makes hosting the party a joy, not an overwhelming task.

Share the Costs

Mother Angelica said that family life, the backbone of mankind, is dependent on giving, sharing, and receiving from each other. Do not argue about money. Respect and honor each family member's financial contributions, no matter how small.

Work out funding solutions that fit your family. In the early years of the Raezer Christmas party, we asked each person to bring something. As the number of family members grew, we found it increasingly difficult to make the food logistics work. Although our kitchen has a double oven, we could neither heat nor cook simultaneously all the lunch and dinner offerings that everyone brought to share. We needed to implement a different plan.

We decided to have the Christmas party catered. We would split the catering costs among the family members. When we asked each member to provide an equal share, however, we found that this principle did not work. We hadn't considered that some had driven many hours and traveled great distances to be there. It wasn't fair to ask these family members to participate in catering the party. Their presence was their contribution. For others, the catering fee simply exacted an undue financial burden. We realized that taking this approach would discourage many from attending, and this was unacceptable.

What then transpired was incredible and comforting. Three family members decided to cover the catering costs. Their handling of the money conundrum restored the focus of the Christmas party to the joy of getting together.

You want to avoid losing a family member simply because the burden you put on them is too big. Find a way that all family members can contribute to the event and encourage those with more resources to take on a larger share.

Gather Feedback About Your Annual Event and Implement Improvements

It is extremely important to get feedback from the people who have attended your annual event. Our Christmas party has been fine-tuned over twenty years. The best scheduling was worked out, the best way to fund the party was worked out, the food sources were worked out, the songbook was worked out, and the activity timetables were worked out in the first couple of years by trying something, making changes, and trying again.

From there, there has been just minimal tweaking every year. If the salads largely go uneaten but there is not enough lasagna, that is noted and adjusted for next year. The party start time has changed many times as families with young children have requested earlier and earlier starts. A member suggested that more trash receptacles be made available so that each member could easily dispose of their own drinks and paper products, thereby reducing the cleanup effort. Members have also suggested adding new children's songs to our family songbook as well as some adult choices.

Your experience of the party will help you identify changes that need to be made. Additionally, these questions will jog your thinking:

> Did everyone enjoy the event?

> Did we have the right choices of drinks and were there enough?

> Did people enjoy the hors d'oeuvres and were there enough?

> Was the caterer on time and did they provide great food?

> Were takeout or individually purchased dishes delicious?

> Did the choice of foods work for everyone?

> Did the children enjoy the food?

> Was the music appropriate and enjoyed?

> Were the small children engaged in activities?

> Were the event activities enjoyed?

> Were the activities conducive to bonding?

> Did the timetable of activities work well?

- ➤ Did anyone feel rushed?

- ➤ Did anything go wrong?

- ➤ Are there any ideas for improvement?

When people call to say thank you, it is an opportunity for you to ask what can be done to improve the party. Take their suggestions seriously. Your welcoming of feedback and willingness to make changes will be bonding in itself. Your family knows that you care.

Overcoming Threats to the Celebrating Family

The threats to family bonding are many. In this book, we have elected to focus on the internal ones. We have already discussed how relationships have a natural rhythm of connection. If contact were to break off, it is a clear threat to bonding. If a family member does something hurtful and forgiveness is withheld, bonding is broken. Miscommunications and misunderstandings are always a concern and point out the need for heart-to-heart discussion and empathic listening to restore good connection.

We often hear of family events that are disrupted by members seeking control or wielding power. Timothy Keller, in his book *God's Wisdom for Navigating Life*, and in his study of Galatians, identifies the addictions that motivate their behavior: for those seeking control they need everything to be their plan as their greatest nightmare is uncertainty and for those seeking power, they often put someone down to avoid humiliation and/or boost themselves. Timothy Keller identifies two additional addictions that people mistakenly use to establish their worth instead of looking up. He speaks of those seeking approval who will lie to avoid rejection and those seeking comfort to avoid stress and suffering and in so doing complain often and are less productive than they should be.

An understanding of these addictions can help us to forgive and forgive again. Understanding, however, begins with looking inside. It is easier to see the truth of those close to us than the truth about ourselves. We are all prone to having these areas of vulnerability that can cause us to hurt others. When we come to grips with our own weakness and can forgive ourselves for imperfection, we can forgive other's humanity as well.

When you have a Celebrating Family, your family's greatest risk is the loss of family bonds. Take good care to protect them and keep them strong.

Conclusion

George Bernard Shaw described a happy family as an earlier heaven. Those who want a family want a celebrating one, and this goal is attainable. It is achieved by those families that adopt our eight-step program. Celebrating Families put the required skills and principles to work effectively. This commitment produces respectful and loving interactions among all its members.

Celebrating Families set a rhythm of ongoing close contact and prioritize their time to be available to other members. Family members develop a set of unique strategies to meet their bonding objectives consistent with the makeup and experience of their members. They learn to work as a team to share the work and develop methods to cover the costs of an annual family event.

A highly recommended part of the annual event is Circle Time, which provides a powerful way to build closeness and unity. The same is true for the use of a family sing supported by a family songbook.

When you have achieved your goal of creating a Celebrating Family, you have life's greatest gift. Celebrating

Families produce loving and productive children, the greatest form of wealth. It is this wealth, when passed on to future generations, that ensures the longevity of your family. Celebrating Families exist because a group of committed family members will them to be so.

They also make a contribution to America. As families are restored across America, they reinforce America's constitutional republic with its focus on individual freedom and the preservation of each citizen's inalienable rights: life, liberty, and the pursuit of happiness.

Acknowledgments

Thanks to Tim Neilson, Anthony Capriotti, and Susan Fedoris for their time spent reviewing our proposed steps and their thoughtful suggestions.

Thank you to our first readers, Charlyn Marcley, Sue Wenger, Tim Neilson, and Nick Ruben, for the time they took to read and understand our book and share their powerful insights. Thank you to Patty Grier Kirschner for her gift of an extensive and invaluable edit of our manuscript.

We are so appreciative for the help our developmental editor, Katherine Pickett, gave us. Thank you to our full publication team, Steve Harrison, Cristina Smith, Valerie Costa, Christy Day, Steve Scholl and Maggie McLaughlin.

Bibliography

Blackney, Raymond B. *Meister Eckhart: A Modern Translation.* New York: Harper and Brothers, 1941.

Blanchard, Kenneth and Spencer Johnson. *The One Minute Manager.* New York: William Morrow & Company, 1982.

de Tocqueville, Alexis. *Democracy in America Volume 1 and 2.* New York: Vintage Books, 1960.

Goleman, Daniel. *Emotional Intelligence.* New York: Random House Publishing, 2005.

Keller, Timothy. *Galatians: Living in Line with the Truth of the Gospel.* New York: Redeemer Presbyterian Church, 2003

Keller, Timothy and Kathy Keller. *God's Wisdom for Navigating Life: A Year of Daily Devotions in the Book of Proverbs.* New York: Viking, 2017

King, Jr., Martin Luther. *The Words of Martin Luther King, Jr.* New York: New Market Press, 1996.

Kraybill, Donald B., Steven M. Nolt, and David L. Weaver-Zerche. *Amish Grace: How Forgiveness Transcended Tragedy.* San Francisco: Jossey-Bass, 2010.

Ozment, Steven. *A Mighty Fortress: A New History of the German People.* New York: Harper-Collins Publishers, 2004.

Peterson, Christopher, Steven Maier, and Martin Seligman. *Learned Helplessness: A Theory for the Age of Personal Control.* New York, Oxford University Press, 1993.

Putnam, Robert D. *Bowling Alone: The Collapse and Revival of American Community.* New York, Simon & Schuster, 2000.

Raezer, John. *Supporting an Instinct for Growth.* White Paper 2014.

Ruben, Nick. *How to be a World-Class Listener: Connect with People in Ways You Never Thought Possible.* Morrisville: Lulu Publishing, 2016.

Seligman, Martin. *Authentic Happiness: Using the new Positive Psychology to Realize Your Potential for lasting Fulfillment.* New York: Atria Books, 2004.

Suzuki, Shinichi. *Nurtured by Love: The Classic Approach to Talent Education.* Princeton: Alfred Publishing Company, 1993.

About the Authors

John's Background

John Raezer completed his undergraduate studies at Harvard and went on to do his masters and doctoral studies in Economics at the University of Pennsylvania. He taught at Villanova, UPenn's Executive Education Program, NYU, and summer programs at Dartmouth, Stanford, and Williams. He lectured on Risk Management all over the world. His personal life was in a shambles before he married Sallie.

Sallie's Background

Sallie Raezer graduated from Bucknell University where she majored in music. She went on to study piano performance with Alexander Fiorillo, Vladimir Horowitz's student, for eight years. Sallie trained to be a Systems Engineer, and then did systems projects for Standard and Poor's, Dupont, Sun Oil, and Miller, Anderson, Sherrerd among others. Her personal life was falling apart before she married John.

Together

John and Sallie shared a burning desire to straighten out their lives and have a happy family. They began a study of family bonding, and this book is the result of their thirty year journey. They achieved their dream of a Celebrating Family. In The Celebrating Family, they share the eight steps that transformed their family. Currently they live in the Philadelphia area. They love get-togethers with family and friends, music, eating well, following their sports teams, going to the theater, and visiting the Jersey shore.

The Raezers can be reached by email at TheCelebratingFamily@gmail.com or through their website, TheCelebratingFamily.com.

Made in the USA
Middletown, DE
16 July 2023

35194224R00076